Ter
from the

ex libris

Candlestick Press

Published by:

Candlestick Press,
Diversity House, 72 Nottingham Road, Arnold, Nottingham NG5 6LF
www.candlestickpress.co.uk

Design and typesetting by Craig Twigg

Printed by Ratcliff & Roper Print Group, Nottinghamshire, UK

Selection and Introduction © Seán Hewitt, 2021

Cover illustration © Sam Cannon, 2021
www.samcannonart.co.uk

Candlestick Press monogram © Barbara Shaw, 2008

© Candlestick Press, 2021
Reprinted 2022

ISBN 978 1 907598 93 7

Acknowledgements

The poems in this pamphlet are reprinted from the following books, all by
permission of the publishers listed unless stated otherwise. Every effort has been
made to trace the copyright holders of the poems published in this book. The
editor and publisher apologise if any material has been included without
permission or without the appropriate acknowledgement, and would be glad to be
told of anyone who has not been consulted.

Thanks are due to all the copyright holders cited below for their kind permission:

Kayo Chingonyi, *Kumukanda* (Chatto & Windus, 2017) by permission of
Penguin Random House UK; Helen Dunmore, *Counting Backwards: Poems
1975-2017* (Bloodaxe Books, 2019) www.bloodaxebooks.com; WD Ehrhart,
Thank You for Your Service: Collected Poems, (McFarland & Company, Inc.,
2019) by kind permission of the author and publisher; Vona Groarke, *Spindrift*
(Gallery Press, 2009) by kind permission of the author and The Gallery Press,
Loughcrew, Oldcastle, County Meath, Ireland; Jen Hadfield, *Nigh-No-Place*
(Bloodaxe Books, 2008) www.bloodaxebooks.com; Seán Hewitt, first published
here, by kind permission of the author; Vita Sackville-West, *The Land*,
reproduced with permission of Curtis Brown Group Ltd, London on behalf of the
Beneficiaries of the Estate of Vita Sackville-West. Copyright © Vita Sackville-
West 1926.

All permissions cleared courtesy of Swift Permissions
swiftpermissions@gmail.com

Where poets are no longer living their dates are given.

Contents

Introduction

The countryside is perhaps the place, above all others, that we associate with poetry. In the ten poems I have chosen for this pamphlet, you'll encounter landscapes across the UK, Ireland and further afield, written by poets working over the past two centuries. There are beautiful lyric poems, love poems, poems about birth and death, and poems about all sorts of birds and animals. What connects them is a love of nature, a love of the land, and an awareness of the eclectic ways we think of ourselves as belonging to it.

As you might expect, these poems are governed by the changing seasons. We begin with the surprising exuberance of John Clare's frozen heath in winter, right through to the abundance of Helen Dunmore's miraculous field. We meet "a farmer of dreams"; we are called to the waters of a loch; we meet a robin, whose song confounds poetry itself.

In these poems, we are also reminded that the countryside is difficult, imperilled, the source of both pastoral idyll (as in the extract from Vita Sackville-West's *The Land*) and national myth. In Jen Hadfield's brilliant 'Hüm', the poet's Shetland is full of toil, and the wild exhilaration of the elements. The countryside, for these poets, is place of labour and of love; but it is also a place imbued with memory, with loss, and with chance encounters and hauntings.

This pamphlet is full of songs, and the musicality of the natural world shines through them at every turn. It's my hope that you'll enjoy these poems as much as I do, and that they will remind you (if, indeed, you need reminding) of the importance of the precious and precarious world we are lucky enough to live in.

Seán Hewitt

Emmonsail's Heath in Winter

I love to see the old heath's withered brake
Mingle its crimpled leaves with furze and ling,
While the old heron from the lonely lake
Starts slow and flaps his melancholy wing,
And oddling crow in idle motions swing
On the half-rotten ash tree's topmost twig,
Beside whose trunk the gipsy makes his bed.
Up flies the bouncing woodcock from the brig
Where a black quagmire quakes beneath the tread;
The fieldfares chatter in the whistling thorn
And for the haw round fields and closen rove,
And coy bumbarrels, twenty in a drove,
Flit down the hedgerows in the frozen plain
And hang on little twigs and start again.

John Clare (1793 – 1864)

After the Winter

Some day, when trees have shed their leaves
    And against the morning's white
The shivering birds beneath the eaves
    Have sheltered for the night,
We'll turn our faces southward, love,
    Toward the summer isle
Where bamboos spire the shafted grove
    And wide-mouthed orchids smile.

And we will seek the quiet hill
    Where towers the cotton tree,
And leaps the laughing crystal rill,
    And works the droning bee.
And we will build a cottage there
    Beside an open glade,
With black-ribbed blue-bells blowing near,
    And ferns that never fade.

Claude McKay (1889 – 1948)

On the South Downs

Over the downs there were birds flying,
    Far off glittered the sea,
And toward the north the weald of Sussex
    Lay like a kingdom under me.

I was happier than the larks
    That nest on the downs and sing to the sky –
Over the downs the birds flying
    Were not so happy as I.

It was not you, though you were near,
    Though you were good to hear and see,
It was not earth, it was not heaven,
    It was myself that sang in me.

Sara Teasdale (1884 – 1933)

The Farmer

Each day I go into the fields to see what is growing
and what remains to be done.
It is always the same thing: nothing
is growing, everything needs to be done.
Plow, harrow, disc, water, pray
till my bones ache and hands rub
blood-raw with honest labor –
all that grows is the slow
intransigent intensity of need.
I have sown my seed on soil
guaranteed by poverty to fail.
But I don't complain – except
to passersby who ask me why
I work such barren earth.
They would not understand me
if I stooped to lift a rock
and hold it like a child, or laughed,
or told them it is their poverty
I labor to relieve. A farmer of dreams
knows how to pretend. A farmer of dreams
knows what it means to be patient.
Each day I go into the fields.

WD Ehrhart

Hüm (noun)
(for Bo)

Twilight, gloaming;
to walk blind
against the wind;

to be abject; lick snot
and rain from the top lip
like a sick calf.

To be blinded by rain
from the north.

To be blinded
by westerly rain.

To walk uphill
into a tarry peatcut
and bluster a deal
with the Trowes.

To cross the bull's field
in the dark.

To pass in the dark
a gate of hollow bars
inside which the wind is broaling.

To pass in the dark
a byre like a rotten walnut.

To not know the gate
till you run up against it.

Jen Hadfield

Spring in Hartsop

As though God had risen above the fells
and shown his face, the earth answered...
So long since the sun broke the clouds

or the hills shone in their veil of air,
and now the thorn, unturning its clusters,
its spokes of flower – the snowdrops

pushing in rings like choirs, each tilting
its neck, ready to sing. Since you left, I too
have slept in the dark of my body's

wintering; but now, by the window,
I can feel my heart hatching; your hand,
gentle, lifting my head to the sun.

Seán Hewitt

An Teach Tuí

Thistledown, fuchsia, flagstone floor:
this noun house has the wherewithal
to sit out centuries

squat between bog-water darkness
and rooms turned inside out to summer,

straw-coloured months of childhood
answering each other

like opposite windows
in thick-set walls

that sunlight will cajole.

Tea roses bluster the half-door.
Rain from eaves footfalls the gravel.

A robin, cocksure of himself,
frittered away all morning in the shrub.

If I knew how to fix in even one language
the noise of his wings in flight

I wouldn't need another single word.

Vona Groarke

from **The Land**

The country habit has me by the heart,
For he's bewitched forever who has seen,
Not with his eyes but with his vision, Spring
Flow down the woods and stipple leaves with sun,
As each man knows the life that fits him best,
The shape it makes in his soul, the tune, the tone,
And after ranging on a tentative flight
Stoops like the merlin to the constant lure.
The country habit has me by the heart.
I never hear the sheep-bells in the fold,
Nor see the ungainly heron rise and flap
Over the marsh, nor hear the asprous corn
Clash, as the reapers set the sheaves in shocks
(That like a tented army dream away
The night beneath the moon in silvered fields),
Nor watch the stubborn team of horse and man
Graven upon the skyline, nor regain
The sign-posts on the roads towards my home
Bearing familiar names – without a strong
Leaping of recognition; only here
Lies peace after uneasy truancy;
Here meet and marry many harmonies,
– All harmonies being ultimately one, –
Small mirroring majestic; for as earth
Rolls on her journey, so her little fields
Ripen or sleep, and the necessities
Of seasons match the planetary law.
So truly stride between the earth and heaven
Sowers of grain: so truly in the spring
Earth's orbit swings both blood and sap to rhythm,
And infinite and humble are at one;
So the brown hedger, through the evening lanes
Homeward returning, sees above the ricks,
Sickle in hand, the sickle in the sky.

Vita Sackville-West (1892 – 1962)

Loch Long by Ardgartan, Argyll

Where night is a crow
troubling the surface of the water
and the light of morning
is the breadth of a lover's gaze
and the loch-side mist
gives you back to landscape
I'll wait for you.

Where headlights are slow fish
swimming miles of cobbled river
and this cigarette's glow
is the effortless grace of a firefly
and your troubles are bright
as paper lanterns given to the sky
by fire, you'll find me.

Where the ends of the earth
are the view from a cabin window
and the past is an old song
nobody knows how to sing anymore
and this moment is sudden rain
soaking you through to the skin
I'll meet you.

Kayo Chingonyi

Crossing the field

To live your life is not as simple as to cross a field.
            - Russian Proverb

To cross the field on a sunset of spider-webs
sprung and shining, thistle heads
white with tufts that are harvest
tended and brought to fruit by no one,

to cross the long field as the sun goes down
and the whale-back Scillies show damson
twenty miles off, as the wind sculls
out back, and five lighthouses
one by one open their eyes,

to cross the long field as it darkens
when rooks are homeward, and gulls
swing out from the tilt of land
to the breast of ocean – now is the time
the vixen stirs, and the green lane's
vivid with footprints.

A field is enough to spend a life in.
Harrow, granite and mattress springs,
shards and bones, turquoise droppings
from pigeons that gorge on nightshade berries,
a charm of goldfinch, a flight of linnets,
fieldare and January redwing
venturing westward in the dusk,
all are folded in the dark of the field,

all are folded into the dark of the field
and need more days
to paint them, than life gives.

Helen Dunmore (1952 – 2017)